HOWL LIKE
A WOLF
Animal Proverbs

HOWL LIKE A WOLF

Animal Proverbs

Wolfgang Mieder

Silhouettes by Chris Cart

The New England Press
Shelburne, Vermont

For additional copies of this book or for a catalog of
our other titles, please write:

The New England Press
P.O. Box 575
Shelburne, VT 05482

Contents

CONTENTS

Introduction

Animals have always been an important part of life for humans. They both threatened and sustained early civilizations as people struggled to gain control over the fauna of the world. The animals *were* controlled, then overrun, so now many of the remaining wild animals must be protected in natural parks or zoos. Some animals have also been domesticated, with the result that they have become part of everyday human life on farms or as pets in the home. Whether wild or tame, however, animals have played a significant role in human history.

Many ancient myths, folk tales, fables, and literary works include animals, clearly indicating that they occupy a major position in our social and psychological world view. While it is possible to understand such writings as literal accounts of animal behavior, it is also clear that animal stories are symbolic narratives. Thus Aesop's fables do in fact tell us about the nature of the cunning fox or rapacious wolf, for example, but the animal imagery is also a colorful representation of human traits. Over time, longer tales have been reduced to succinct proverbs that summarize human behavior in short, easily remembered poetic structures. Many additional proverbs were coined simply by watching natural phenomena and realizing that there is a considerable amount of congruity between the lives of animals and humans. The result is literally thousands of concise proverbs that are based on generations of experience and observation.

Animal proverbs are thus literal statements commenting on the behavior of the animals themselves while at the same time expressing similar human behavioral traits in a symbolic or metaphorical fashion. The proverb "Big fish eat little fish," for example, describes an event that occurs in the waters of the world all the time. However, the proverb is also a metaphorical statement on the greedy or overpowering nature of certain people, institutions, or governments. Rather than saying that the dictatorial powers of a particular nation have overrun a smaller and weaker country, a journalist might choose this indirect proverbial statement for a headline relating to this event. Every reader would have a clear mental picture of how this small country was swallowed up against its will by a powerful foe.

Animal proverbs are used throughout the world, and they reflect on some of the most common characteristics of life. But while two proverbs from different cultures might express the same idea, they will use different animal images. It is not surprising then to find elephants and lions more frequently used in African proverbs, while such domesticated animals as dogs and cats take on a more prominent role in European proverbs.

It is also understandable that those animals that have enjoyed a long relationship with humans appear with a higher frequency in proverbs. This is particularly true for such animals as birds, cats, cows, dogs, horses, and a few other domesticated animals. For this reason the chapters for these animals are longer than those for most wild animals.

The twenty-nine chapters of this book have been arranged alphabetically according to the animals of the proverbs. While most of them deal with specific animals, there are also more generic chapters. For birds and snakes, for example, there are proverbs about particular species like the nightingale or the boa constrictor, but most of the proverbs in common parlance use the more general terms. There are, of course, also such distinctions as apes and monkeys, asses and donkeys, frogs and toads, hares and rabbits, and pigs and hogs, but those have been assembled under one chapter in each case. Together the approximately 575 proverbs included in this book represent a selection of the most colorful and frequently used animal proverbs from around the world. Their poetic structures and their animal metaphors are at times amazingly similar or strikingly different, yet the basic ideas expressed in them add up to an insightful commentary on animal and human behavior. While they teach us something about the natural world, they can also teach us much about ourselves.

ANTS

The little ant at its hole is full of courage.
(African-Bemba)

If ants have food the ship will go safely.
(Indian-Marathi)

Ants also have their anger.
(French)

Where the sugar is, there the
ants will also be.
(Philippine)

An ant is over six feet tall when measured
by its own foot-rule.
(Slovenian)

Don't even step on an ant.
(Greek)

An ant hole may collapse
an embankment.
(Japanese)

The tiny ant dares to enter the lion's ear.
(Armenian)

He who cannot pick up an ant and wants
to pick up an elephant will some
day see his folly.
(African-Jabo)

Even an ant casts a shadow.
(Montenegrin)

The ant does not labor in vain.
(German)

A very little water is a sea to an ant.
(Pashto)

Many ants kill a camel.
(Turkish)

Any spoke will lead the ant to the hub.
(American)

Consider the ant, you sluggard,
and be wise.
(English)

Good firewood is not without ants.
(African-Cameroons)

Though the enemy be only like an ant,
regard him like an elephant.
(Danish)

Even the ant has its bite.
(Turkish)

What hundred ants built, one ass
tears down.
(German)

APES
(MONKEYS)

When you see a monkey on a tree, it has
already seen you.
(African-Fulani)

An old ape never made a pretty grimace.
(French)

The higher the ape goes, the more he
shows his tail.
(English)

An old monkey does not learn dancing.
(Moroccan)

Monkey see, monkey do.
(American)

As the parent monkey chatters,
so does its young.
(Philippine)

Apes are never more beasts than when
they wear men's clothes.
(English)

An ape, a priest, and a louse, are three
devils in one house.
(Dutch)

However foolish the monkey, it will not
play with the thorn tree.
(African-Hausa)

There is no ape who doesn't swear that
he has the handsomest children.
(German)

Even a monkey may sometimes fall
from the tree.
(Korean)

One monkey does not like another
to get a bellyful.
(African-Efik)

An ape is an ape, though clad in purple.
(English)

ASSES
(DONKEYS)

An ass does not stumble twice over
the same stone.
(French)

It's better be carried by an ass than
thrown by a horse.
(Dutch)

Bucking will not rid a donkey of a load.
(African-Hausa)

The ass brays when he pleases.
(English)

A hungry ass eats any straw.
(Italian)

When an ass bears too light a load he
wants to lie down.
(Russian)

Everybody beats the donkey that
has no owner.
(Turkish)

A donkey is a donkey though it may
carry the Sultan's treasure.
(Lebanese)

Make yourself an ass, and everyone will
lay his sack on you.
(German)

They don't unload the caravan for one
lame donkey.
(Iranian)

A contented ass enjoys a long life.
(Portuguese)

No ass is lazy when teased
by the manger.
(Mexican)

A donkey that travels abroad will not
return a horse.
(Hebrew)

Asses carry the oats and horses eat them.
(Dutch)

If you are born an ass, you will die one.
(Hebrew)

A thistle is a fat salad for an ass's mouth.
(English)

An ass is most pleasing to another ass.
(Slovakian)

The ass and his driver do not think alike.
(German)

For a stubborn ass a stubborn driver.
(French)

The ass that has not enough strength
throws down his pack saddle.
(Turkish)

Two donkeys together will act alike
and smell alike.
(Iranian)

Every ass loves to hear himself bray.
(English)

Only a donkey is patient under a load.
(African-Hausa)

You can recognize a donkey by his long
ears, a fool by his long tongue.
(Yiddish)

The braying of an ass does not
reach heaven.
(Italian)

The hungry ass runs more strongly
than the horse.
(Turkish)

Though the ass may carry a sack of gold,
it nevertheless feeds on thistles.
(Danish)

Asses must not be tied up with horses.
(French)

When the donkey has it too good he
will dance on the ice.
(German)

The masses are asses.
(Yiddish)

BEARS

Two bears don't live together
in one den.
(Russian)

The bear thinks one thing, and his
leader thinks another.
(English)

A hungry bear does not play.
(Turkish)

Bear and bull catch no fox.
(German)

A bear that is not tied up won't dance.
(Russian)

Don't play with the bear if you don't
want to be bitten.
(Italian)

The bear doesn't dance for his
own pleasure.
(Rumanian)

Don't make the bear the keeper
of the honey.
(German)

He who has taken the bear into the boat
must cross over with him.
(Swedish)

The bear dances, but the keeper takes
the money.
(Russian)

Don't sell the skin of the bear that's
still in the forest.
(Yiddish)

When one flees from the wolf
the bear appears.
(Finnish)

Time to catch bears is when they're out.
(American)

BEES

One bee is better than a thousand flies.
(Spanish)

A bee is never caught in a shower.
(English)

Beware of a man's shadow and
a bee's sting.
(Burmese)

It takes a bee to get the sweetness out
of the blossom.
(American)

Bees do not become hornets.
(French)

One bee does not make a swarm.
(German)

Where bees are there is honey.
(English)

The wise bee does not sip from a flower
that has fallen.
(Chinese)

Honey is sweet, but the bee stings.
(English)

He who wants to eat honey should bear
the sting of bees.
(Lebanese)

There is no bee without a
hidden stinger.
(Dutch)

No bees, no honey; no work, no money.
(American)

Where the bee does not find any flowers
it sits down on thistles.
(German)

The busy bee has no time for sadness.
(French)

BIRDS

The bird that escapes from the cage
never wants to come back.
(Vietnamese)

Where there are birds there is water.
(African-Ovambo)

It's an ill bird that fouls its own nest.
(English)

A bird never flew so high that it did not
come to the ground for food.
(Dutch)

Let every bird sing his own note.
(Danish)

It is a brave bird that makes its nest
in the cat's ear.
(Indian-Hindi)

It is the beautiful bird that we put
in the cage.
(Chinese)

As the old birds sing, the young
ones twitter.
(German)

Two birds of prey do not keep each
other company.
(Spanish)

Birds of a feather flock together.
(English)

The late bird shakes its wings; the early
one wipes its bill.
(Estonian)

Every bird admires its own nest.
(Turkish)

The bird seeks the tree, not the
tree the bird.
(Mexican)

When a big bird does not bother to fly it
goes to sleep hungry.
(African-Ashanti)

One bird in the hand is better than ten
on the tree.
(Lebanese)

You can tell a bird by its song and a man
by his manner of speaking.
(Greek)

Young birds do not fly too far.
(Jamaican)

Though a bird is hungry, it will not eat
poisonous berries.
(Indian-Tamil)

A bird in the hand is worth two
in the bush.
(English)

Little by little the bird builds its nest.
(French)

It is hard to catch birds with
an empty hand.
(German)

A singing bird killed furnishes no meat.
(Chinese)

A bird that has been hurt by an arrow
will be frightened even by a
crooked twig.
(Korean)

A big bird cannot be trapped with chaff.
(African-Shona)

The bird flies not without cause.
(Turkish)

Old birds are not caught with new nets.
(Italian)

The bird is not big until he spreads
his wings.
(African-Jabo)

The early bird catches the worm.
(English)

Birds of prey do not sing.
(German)

A caged bird longs for the clouds.
(Japanese)

CAMELS

The camel carries the burden, the dog
does the panting.
(Turkish)

The camel does not see his own hump.
(Armenian)

Once the camel gets his nose into the
tent his body will soon follow.
(Egyptian)

The last straw breaks the camel's back.
(English)

As the camel, so the load.
(Hebrew)

The camel that leads the file pays no
attention to the rear.
(Turkish)

Some think they are giants when they sit
on the hump of a camel.
(Russian)

The camel wants one thing and the
camel driver wants another.
(Lebanese)

A camel with bells is not lost.
(Turkish)

A mangy camel bears the load
of many camels.
(Greek)

Old camels carry the skins of the young
ones to the market.
(Egyptian)

A camel that wants fodder stretches
out its neck.
(Iranian)

You don't water a camel with a spoon.
(Armenian)

CATS

It is better to feed one cat
than many mice.
(Norwegian)

Curiosity killed the cat.
(English)

What is play to the cat is death
to the mouse.
(Danish)

At night all cats are grey.
(German)

He who is born a cat will run after mice.
(French)

A cat and a rat cannot be kept at
the same place.
(African-Shona)

The cat likes fish but she doesn't want
to wet her paws.
(Yiddish)

The cat is friendly, but it scratches.
(Spanish)

A cat with gloves will catch no mice.
(Armenian)

He who begrudges the cat's food finds
his clothes eaten by the mice.
(Greek)

A cat is heavy if carried constantly.
(Irish)

He who hunts with cats will catch mice.
(Danish)

When the cat and mouse agree, the
grocer is ruined.
(Iranian)

Small cats catch small mice.
(Vietnamese)

The cat and dog may kiss, yet are none
the better friends.
(English)

Two cats and one mouse, two women in
one house, two dogs to one bone will
not agree long.
(German)

He who does not keep a cat keeps mice.
(Serbian)

Cat and mouse cannot be
neighbors long.
(African-Ovambo)

A meowing cat can't catch mice.
(Yiddish)

An old cat likes young mice.
(Greek)

When the cat's away the mice will play.
(English)

When the cat dies, the mice rejoice.
(African-Oji)

The scalded cat fears cold water.
(English)

He who denies the cat skimmed milk
must give the mouse cream.
(Russian)

He who wants to play with a cat should
be able to bear its scratches.
(Lebanese)

The dream of the cat is all
about the mice.
(Egyptian)

The cats that drive away mice are as
good as those that catch them.
(German)

A bashful cat makes a proud mouse.
(Scottish)

When the cat has gone, the rats come
out to stretch themselves.
(Chinese)

A cat is a lion to a mouse.
(Albanian)

CHICKENS
(HENS)

Not even a chicken digs for nothing.
(Czech)

Hens that cackle much lay few eggs.
(Estonian)

A hen does not break her own egg.
(African-Swahili)

Better a chicken today than
a goose tomorrow.
(German)

The chicken that stays at home picks
up the crumbs.
(Portuguese)

Don't count your chickens before
they are hatched.
(English)

If you get mixed in with bran you'll soon
be pecked by chickens.
(Libyan)

Out of a white egg comes a black chick.
(Italian)

A chicken does not crow in the presence
of a rooster.
(African-Swahili)

The old hen is worth forty chickens.
(Greek)

My chicken is good, but my neighbor's
looks better.
(Rumanian)

It is a bad hen that eats at your house
and lays at another's.
(Spanish)

Better a chicken in the hand than an
eagle in the sky.
(Yiddish)

Chickens will come home to roost.
(English)

The chicken is no match for the knife.
(African-Swahili)

A black hen will lay a white egg.
(English)

The hen lays an egg, and the cock feels
pain in his bottom.
(Moroccan)

No one sells his laying hen without
a good reason.
(African-Ashanti)

A hen pecks one grain at a time and lives
with a full stomach.
(Russian)

The rooster can crow, but it's the hen
that delivers the goods.
(American)

COWS

Though the cow gives a large pot of
milk, it is not equal to the horse
in speed.
(Indian-Tamil)

The calf belongs to the owner
of the cow.
(Irish)

You cannot get two skins from one cow.
(Chinese)

Though a cow wanders here and there it
does not trample its young.
(African-Ovambo)

A cow from afar gives plenty of milk.
(French)

When one cow has started to move it
raises the others from their rest.
(African-Ovambo)

He who will steal a calf will steal a cow.
(English)

Better one cow in the stable than ten
in the field.
(Yiddish)

A cow never goes so far that her tail
does not follow.
(Norwegian)

An affectionate calf gets to suck
two cows.
(Russian)

You cannot sell the cow and have
the milk too.
(English)

A cow does not know the value of its
tail until it is cut off.
(African-Swahili)

The laggard cow gets the sour grass.
(Danish)

Black cows give white milk.
(German)

An old cow does not remember
having been a calf.
(Finnish)

To get milk and eggs you must not
frighten the cow and hen.
(Tibetan)

Where the cow is, there is her calf.
(Indian-Hindi)

If you love the cow you will love the calf.
(Jamaican)

The world is your cow, but you have
to do the milking.
(American)

A cow among calves does not grow old.
(African-Ovambo)

Milk the cow, but don't pull
off the udder.
(Dutch)

CROWS

One crow does not make a winter.
(Dutch)

A whitewashed crow will not remain
white long.
(Chinese)

From a crow's beak comes
a crow's voice.
(Greek)

Crows are black the whole world over.
(English)

As the crow is, so is its egg.
(Philippine)

A once frightened crow is even
afraid of a bush.
(Russian)

When the crows sing the nightingales
fly away.
(Greek)

A crow is never the whiter for
often washing.
(Danish)

A crow in a cage won't talk like a parrot.
(American)

Crows gather where the carrion lies.
(Rumanian)

A flying crow always catches something.
(Dutch)

One crow does not peck out
another's eyes.
(German)

A sitting crow starves.
(Icelandic)

A crow does not lay dove's eggs.
(Greek)

DOGS

A dog has four feet but he can't walk
four different paths.
(Jamaican)

The dog does not know how to swim
until the water reaches his ears.
(Russian)

You cannot teach an old dog new tricks.
(English)

An old dog does not bark for nothing.
(French)

A dog lying down has surrendered.
(African-Shona)

If you have stepped over the dog, step
over its tail too.
(Estonian)

Every dog barks differently.
(Slovakian)

A dog is sometimes more faithful
than a child.
(Yiddish)

A good dog deserves a good bone.
(English)

Do not give the dog bread every time
he wags his tail.
(Italian)

He who yaps like a dog will be beaten
like a dog.
(Polish)

After a time even a dog makes a
compromise with the cat.
(Hungarian)

The dog barks at the moon all night
long, but the moon never hears him.
(Rumanian)

A mad dog bites anything but himself.
(Libyan)

The starving dog fears not the stick.
(Japanese)

He who lies down with dogs will
rise with fleas.
(English)

A dog barking at a shadow will set a
hundred dogs to bark in unison.
(Korean)

The dog with many homes
dies of hunger.
(Slovakian)

Anyone who sees a leopard knows
it is not a dog.
(African-Hausa)

If the dog goes when the cat comes,
there will be no fight.
(Chinese)

An old dog cannot be taught to sit up.
(Burmese)

Let sleeping dogs lie.
(English)

A dog who barks too often leads the
wolf to the sheep.
(Armenian)

A dog does not take it ill when he is
hit with bread.
(Finnish)

Dogs do not bark at a dead wolf.
(Rumanian)

If the dog is patted on the head,
it wags its tail.
(Philippine)

Every dog has his day.
(English)

Two dogs over one bone seldom agree.
(German)

He who associates with dogs
learns to pant.
(Russian)

A dog is man's best friend.
(English)

The dog barks and the caravan passes on.
(Turkish)

ELEPHANTS

Where an elephant is being killed,
nobody notices the death of a monkey.
(African-Hausa)

Even an elephant may slip.
(Indian-Tamil)

An elephant without a keeper is like
a man without a wife.
(Vietnamese)

It is easy to cut to pieces a dead
elephant, but no one dares to attack
a live one.
(African-Yoruba)

The elephant is not bothered by
the flea bite.
(Italian)

A hair from the head of a woman can
tie up a large elephant.
(Japanese)

Don't act like an elephant in
a china shop.
(German)

An elephant is not burdened by its tusks.
(African-Shona)

An elephant never forgets.
(American)

The elephant is killed because
he has tusks.
(Chinese)

An elephant is not bothered by
sunshine or rain.
(Indian-Tamil)

No one who is following an elephant has
to knock the dew off the grass.
(African-Ashanti)

Tie an elephant with a chicken-tether
and it will break.
(Burmese)

Even elephants will stumble though they
have four feet.
(Malaysian)

If you're going to move, move like an
elephant, not like a hyena.
(African-Hausa)

The elephant is frightened of the gnat.
(Hebrew)

One elephant does not raise a
cloud of dust.
(African-Ovambo)

The world befriends the elephant
and tramples on the ant.
(Indian-Hindustani)

FISH

A fish begins to stink at the head.
(Greek)

Large fish do not live in a small pond.
(Japanese)

The fish sees the bait, not the hook.
(Chinese)

Fry the big fish first and the little
ones afterwards.
(Jamaican)

The fish comes to the rod of the
one who waits.
(Estonian)

A small fish on the table is better than a
big one that still has to be caught.
(Philippine)

He who wants to catch fish must not
mind getting wet.
(Spanish)

Big fish eat little fish.
(English)

The fish in the well experiences
no pleasure.
(African-Hausa)

A fish should swim thrice: in water,
in sauce, and in wine.
(German)

Don't rub your belly when the little
fish is still in the pond.
(Yiddish)

Better a big fish in a little pond than a
little fish in a big pond.
(American)

Fish are not bought at the
bottom of the sea.
(Moroccan)

The sea has fish for every man.
(English)

A fish is caught by its mouth,
a man by his words.
(Philippine)

Don't teach fish how to swim.
(French)

The little fish cannot swallow
the big fish.
(Hawaiian)

Gut no fish until you get it.
(Scottish)

A fish bites best on a silver hook.
(Norwegian)

The fish that escaped is the big one.
(Chinese)

If plain water were satisfying enough,
then the fish would not take the hook.
(African-Ashanti)

There are as good fish in the sea as
ever came out of it.
(English)

Big fish are caught in deep waters.
(Croatian)

Every little fish expects to
become a whale.
(Danish)

Don't bless the fish till it gets
to the land.
(Irish)

Rice and fish are as inseparable as
mother and child.
(Vietnamese)

A little bait catches a big fish.
(Greek)

Fish and company stink in three days.
(English)

A small fish is better than a
large cockroach.
(Russian)

FLIES

A fly does not mind dying
in coconut cream.
(African-Swahili)

Where there is honey, there flies gather.
(Yiddish)

A short tail won't keep off flies.
(Italian)

Flies go to lean horses.
(English)

The fly flutters about the candle till at
last it gets burnt.
(Dutch)

53

Every fly has its shadow.
(Portuguese)

No fly gets into a shut mouth.
(Spanish)

Small flies bother large people.
(German)

Flies will not land on a boiling pot.
(French)

You must lose a fly to catch a trout.
(English)

A fly can drive away horses.
(Greek)

Big flies break the spider's web.
(Italian)

The fly does not kill, but it does spoil.
(Hebrew)

You can catch more flies with molasses
than with vinegar.
(American)

Flies swarm where there is honey.
(Indian-Tamil)

The spider's web lets the rat escape
and catches the fly.
(Spanish)

When a fly does not get up off a dead
body, it is buried with it.
(African-Ashanti)

Let every one keep off the flies
with his own tail.
(Italian)

The busy fly is in every man's dish.
(Spanish)

FOXES

The fox sits but once on a thorn.
(Armenian)

Every fox looks after his own skin.
(Danish)

The fox thinks everybody eats poultry
like himself.
(French)

Don't put the fox to guard
the henhouse.
(English)

A tired fox finds his tail heavy.
(Serbian)

The fox is cunning, but more cunning is
he who catches him.
(Rumanian)

He who would cheat the fox
must rise early.
(Spanish)

When the fox is hungry he pretends
to be asleep.
(Greek)

The old fox does not fear the trap.
(Turkish)

Let every fox take care of his own tail.
(Italian)

When the fox wants to catch geese,
he wags his tail.
(German)

Foxes are caught with foxes.
(Finnish)

A fox does not smell his own stench.
(American)

It is a poor fox that has but one hole.
(German)

When you cannot clothe yourself in the
lion's skin, put on that of the fox.
(Spanish)

Neighbors watch more closely
than foxes.
(Greek)

When the fox dies, the fowls
don't mourn.
(African-Yoruba)

The sleeping fox catches no chickens.
(English)

FROGS
(TOADS)

You can't catch two frogs with one hand.
(Chinese)

A frog likes water but not hot water.
(African-Swahili)

Though you seat the frog on a golden
stool, he'll soon jump off again
into the pool.
(German)

If there is a marsh, there will be frogs.
(Russian)

The frog forgets he was a tadpole.
(Korean)

The frog would like to have wings.
(African-Ovambo)

You can't get feathers of a toad.
(English)

Even a frog would bite if it had teeth.
(Italian)

The frog perishes by its own mouth.
(Indian-Tamil)

A frog can't sing like a nightingale.
(German)

The frog at the bottom of a well believes
that the sky is as small as a lid of
a cooking pot.
(Vietnamese)

A frog wants to make himself as
big as a bull.
(French)

A frog in the well knows not the ocean.
(Japanese)

You can't tell by the looks of a frog how
far he can jump.
(American)

GEESE

What's good for the goose is good
for the gander.
(English)

Roasted geese don't come flying
into your mouth.
(Dutch)

The hen of our neighbors appears
to us as a goose.
(Chinese)

The goose that flies over the sea
returns as a goose.
(German)

When the coop is secure, the geese
will grow fatter.
(Yiddish)

The goose that has lost its head
no longer cackles.
(Danish)

It is a silly goose that comes to
a fox's sermon.
(English)

The goose hisses, but it does not bite.
(Dutch)

Where there are geese, there is cackling.
(Irish)

Feather by feather the goose is plucked.
(Italian)

A goose drinks as much as a gander.
(Swedish)

There is more than one way
to cook a goose.
(American)

A wild goose never lays a tame egg.
(English)

For fame and profit man rushes to a land
which even wild geese do not visit.
(Chinese)

You don't buy any grain from a goose.
(Yiddish)

Falcon with falcon, and goose
with goose.
(Turkish)

A farmer without a wife is worse off than
a goose without water.
(Russian)

A hundred geese will kill a wolf.
(German)

GOATS

A goat is not easy to fence in.
(Norwegian)

The goat learns wisdom from
a cropped ear.
(African-Hausa)

An old goat is never the more revered
for its beard.
(English)

The goat must not deal with the wolf.
(German)

You never saw a goat dying of hunger.
(French)

The goat prefers one goat to
a herd of sheep.
(Armenian)

Better a goat that gives milk than a
pitcher of oil that might spill.
(Egyptian)

No matter how well you clean a goat, it
will still smell like a goat.
(Philippine)

The goat dwells among men for fear
of the leopard.
(African-Jabo)

Everyone fears a goat from in front, a
horse from the rear, and a fool
on every side.
(Yiddish)

The goat eats where it is tied.
(Finnish)

A lame goat takes no siesta.
(American)

Better a goat that gives milk than
a cow that doesn't.
(Estonian)

Any goat can jump over a low fence.
(Polish)

A dead goat does not fear the knife.
(African-Ga)

Don't make the goat into a gardener.
(German)

Where there are no sheep,
the goats are honored.
(Czech)

When the wolf sees the goat, he forgets
about the thunderstorm.
(Russian)

HARES
(RABBITS)

Many hares are hunted who haven't
eaten cabbages.
(Polish)

In small woods may be caught
large hares.
(Dutch)

The hare does not eat the grass
around its burrow.
(Chinese)

You cannot capture luck like rabbits.
(German)

The rabbit always returns to its burrow.
(French)

First catch your rabbit and then
make your stew.
(English)

Even the nibbling rabbit can gorge
itself to death.
(Tibetan)

One catches the hare,
and another eats it.
(German)

Work is no rabbit, it doesn't run away.
(Latvian)

If you chase after two rabbits, you
won't catch even one.
(Russian)

A hare is not caught by sitting down.
(African-Hausa)

The rabbit appears where you
don't expect it.
(Spanish)

If you do what people tell you, you will
fish rabbits in the sea and hunt fish
in the forest.
(Bulgarian)

HORSES

Even four horses cannot pull back what
the tongue has let go.
(Slovakian)

You can lead a horse to water but you
cannot make him drink.
(English)

It's better to ride a good horse for a year
than an ass all your life.
(Dutch)

It's not right for a race horse to despise
the pace of a pony.
(African-Hausa)

An old horse does not forget his path.
(Japanese)

The horse is not judged by the saddle.
(German)

A young foal and an old horse draw
not well together.
(Danish)

One's own spurs and another's horse
make the miles short.
(Italian)

Any water suits a thirsty horse.
(Croatian)

A short horse is soon curried.
(English)

It is better to be a horse than a cart.
(American)

Even a good horse cannot wear
two saddles.
(Chinese)

Once a horse is born, someone will be
found to ride it.
(Hebrew)

A horse is petted just before it is bridled.
(Slovakian)

Even horses die from work.
(Russian)

A weary horse finds even his
tail a burden.
(Czech)

It's better to lose the saddle than the
horse.
(Italian)

Don't look a gift horse in the mouth.
(English)

A bad horse eats as much as a good one.
(Danish)

However old the horse, it is better
than new sandals.
(African-Hausa)

The fast horse soon gets tired.
(Slovakian)

A ragged colt may prove a good horse.
(Scottish)

Spur not a willing horse.
(French)

One must plough with the
horse one has.
(German)

After the horse has been stolen,
the stable door is locked.
(Yiddish)

It is not the horse but the oats that
draw the cart.
(Russian)

When two ride on one horse,
one must sit behind.
(English)

Everyone lays a burden on the
willing horse.
(Irish)

Don't swap horses in the middle
of the stream.
(American)

A horse is not caught with
an empty sack.
(Turkish)

LIONS

When you play with a lion, do not put
your hand in its mouth.
(African-Swahili)

The lion is known by his den.
(Turkish)

A lion's skin is never cheap.
(English)

When the lion roars, the hyena is quiet.
(African-Ovambo)

The lion is vanquished by a fly
buzzing in his ear.
(Armenian)

Let sleeping lions lie!
(Yiddish)

When a lion fails to find meat
it eats grass.
(African-Shona)

You can tell a lion by his claws.
(Greek)

A lion doesn't catch mice.
(Russian)

Lions are never caught with cobwebs.
(American)

Even a weak lion is not bitten by a dog.
(African-Ovambo)

In the heart of every brave man
a lion sleeps.
(Turkish)

The lion is not so fierce as he is painted.
(English)

A dead lion is kicked even by an ass.
(Hungarian)

A captured lion is still a lion.
(German)

The lion does not turn around when a
little dog barks at him.
(Rumanian)

If you live with a lion, wear the skin
of a crocodile.
(African-Swahili)

When the lion is dead the hares jump
upon his carcass.
(Italian)

In time even the lion has to be
satisfied with ants.
(Mongolian)

MICE

Mice cease to fear the cat when
she is old.
(Burmese)

It is a bold mouse that makes her nest
in the cat's ear.
(Danish)

Better a mouse in the pot than no
meat at all.
(English)

One mouse eats the clothes and all the
mice get into trouble.
(Greek)

The mice eat the miser's goods.
(African-Oji)

In her dreams a mouse can frighten a cat.
(Armenian)

The mouse that knows but one hole is
soon caught by the cat.
(Spanish)

Even mice do not go to an empty house.
(Serbian)

Two cannot dine off one mouse.
(Russian)

An old mouse does not eat cheese.
(Maltese)

Don't make yourself a mouse, or the
cat will eat you.
(English)

Small mice also have ears.
(German)

When the mouse laughs at the cat,
there is a hole nearby.
(African-Wolof)

The mouse in its hole is a king.
(Moroccan)

Dead mice feel no cold.
(English)

To a mouse there is no greater
beast than a cat.
(Armenian)

The mouse does not leave the cat's
house with a bellyful.
(Italian)

A mouse can build a home
without timber.
(American)

OXEN

He who drives oxen speaks of oxen.
(Finnish)

The fierce ox becomes tame on
strange ground.
(Spanish)

The ox that ploughs is not
to be muzzled.
(Egyptian)

One blind ox will lead a thousand
oxen astray.
(Indian-Kashmiri)

A calf is not found under an ox.
(Armenian)

79

The ox ploughs the field, and the horse
eats the grain.
(Chinese)

It is not the big oxen that do the
best day's work.
(French)

It all depends on whose ox is gored.
(American)

An ox and an ass don't yoke well to
the same plough.
(Dutch)

The ox is never weary of carrying
his horns.
(Haitian)

The ox will not flee the hare.
(African-Ovambo)

He who ploughs with young oxen
makes crooked furrows.
(German)

The tired ox plants his foot firmly.
(Spanish)

With luck, even your ox will calve.
(Yiddish)

PIGS
(HOGS)

To lazy pigs the ground is always frozen.
(Swedish)

If you saw what the hog ate, you would
never eat hog meat.
(Jamaican)

Don't buy a pig in a poke.
(English)

Old pigs have hard snouts.
(German)

Give a pig a chair, and it'll want to
get on the table.
(Yiddish)

The lazy pig does not eat ripe pears.
(Italian)

Don't strew roses before hogs.
(Dutch)

Where a pig burrows, there are roots.
(Latvian)

The still pig gets all the slop.
(English)

There's no need to grease the fat
hog's rump.
(French)

One pig knows another.
(Irish)

It takes a bushel of corn to fatten
a pig's tail.
(American)

A pig never becomes a sheep.
(Greek)

The worst pig gets the best acorn.
(Spanish)

A clean pig makes lean bacon.
(Serbian)

The young pig grunts like the old sow.
(English)

The hog dreams of its trough.
(Finnish)

He who lies in the sty will be eaten
by the pigs.
(Yiddish)

The pig, when washed, returns
to the muck.
(Czech)

RATS

A cornered rat will bite a cat.
(Japanese)

Don't throw water on a drowned rat.
(English)

One rat is outside but many rats are
inside the hole.
(African-Kpelle)

The rat shows its teeth when crying.
(Hawaiian)

A rat who gnaws at a cat's tail
invites destruction.
(Chinese)

When the rat is caught, it uses its wit.
(German)

Rats never sleep on the mat of the cat.
(African-Jabo)

Rats desert a sinking ship.
(English)

A rat has never lost its hole.
(African-Fulani)

The rat knows a lot, but the cat
knows more.
(German)

Rats know the way of rats.
(Chinese)

It is a poor rat that knows only one hole.
(Swedish)

Married people are like rats in a trap:
they would like to get others into it and
get out themselves.
(Scottish)

Don't ask the rats to watch
over the bacon.
(Dutch)

SHEEP

Counting your sheep won't keep
the wolf away.
(Latvian)

A sheep was never known to
climb a tree.
(Chinese)

It is a silly sheep that confesses
to the wolf.
(Italian)

One bad sheep can easily lead
others astray.
(Philippine)

Do not kill the sheep to take its wool.
(Russian)

A sheep does not give birth to a goat.
(African-Ashanti)

You cannot shear the sheep closer
than the skin.
(Danish)

One sheep follows another.
(English)

The lamb is a sheep in the long run.
(Irish)

Rather lose the wool than the sheep.
(Portuguese)

He who makes himself a sheep will be
eaten by the wolf.
(German)

When one sheep is over the dam,
the rest follow.
(Dutch)

A sheep's bite is never more
than skin deep.
(Italian)

The meek sheep should not try to
imitate a furious bull.
(Tibetan)

When the sheep are shorn,
the lambs tremble.
(Yiddish)

It is easier to take care of sheep
than money.
(Serbian)

The sheep that bleats loses a mouthful.
(Spanish)

There's a black sheep in every family.
(American)

The sheep that is too tame is sucked
by many lambs.
(French)

SNAKES
(SERPENTS)

Big snakes do not live in the same hole.
(African-Ovambo)

Don't trouble a quiet snake.
(Greek)

He who has been bitten by a snake is
afraid of a rope.
(English)

The serpent knows its own hole.
(Chinese)

The snake grows with every repetition
of the story.
(Philippine)

A snake is not killed by its own poison.
(Lebanese)

The snake that wishes to live does not
travel on the highway.
(Haitian)

A serpent, though it is put in a bamboo
tube, won't crawl straight.
(Korean)

He who wants to kill a snake must
aim for its head.
(Danish)

The snake is feared because of its mouth.
(African-Fulani)

If you strike a snake without killing it,
it will turn and bite you.
(Chinese)

Warm up a frozen snake and it will
bite you first.
(Armenian)

He who has been stung by a serpent is
afraid of a lizard.
(Italian)

Kill the snake and save the stick.
(Indian-Bihar)

Fear surrounds the place where a snake
disappeared in the bush.
(African-Jabo)

He who wants to chase away the serpent
must not go barefooted.
(Dutch)

Where the snake enters with the head,
the whole body will follow.
(German)

He who keeps snakes should not be
surprised if he is bitten.
(Czech)

If a snake bites your neighbor,
you too are in danger.
(African-Swahili)

A snake rears snakes.
(Iranian)

WOLVES

Make yourself a sheep, and the
wolf is ready.
(Russian)

It is a hard winter when one
wolf eats another.
(English)

An old wolf does not lose his way.
(Turkish)

A hungry wolf is not at rest.
(Portuguese)

Live with a wolf, howl like a wolf.
(Estonian)

The wolf is not afraid of the dog,
but he hates his bark.
(Yiddish)

When shepherds quarrel, the wolf has
a winning game.
(German)

Do not measure the wolf's tail
till he be dead.
(Serbian)

If the wolf feared rain, he would
wear a cloak.
(Greek)

Where wolves are full, sheep are few.
(Croatian)

One wolf does not bite another.
(Spanish)

The wolf doesn't concern himself with
the price of a sheep.
(African-Hausa)

Wolves of the same litter run in
the same pack.
(American)

Talk of the wolf and you see his tail.
(French)

A sleeping wolf catches no sheep.
(German)

The wolf enters a flock of sheep that
is without a dog.
(Turkish)

Hunger drives the wolf out
of the woods.
(English)

A wolf changes his coat but
never his nature.
(Serbian)

If you're afraid of wolves, don't go
into the forest.
(Russian)

The wolf and the sheep do not agree.
(Turkish)

Where the wolf gets one lamb it
looks for another.
(Spanish)

Little by little the wolf eats the sheep.
(English)

He who keeps company with the wolf
will learn to howl.
(English)

Feed a wolf in the winter and he will
devour you in the summer.
(Greek)

What enters the wolf's throat
is lost forever.
(German)

The hungry wolf goes into the
village for food.
(Lithuanian)

He who wants to wrestle with wolves
must have a bear's claws.
(Swedish)